Personal Introduction: Why This eBook Was Created 3
Introduction 4
   Overview of AI's Role in Society 4
      Brief History of AI 4
   Definition of Open-Source AI 5
      Explanation of Open-Source AI 5
   Thesis Statement 6
   Scope and Objectives 6
Chapter 1: AI Bias and Corporate Influence 7
   Private AI and the Problem of Bias 7
      Argument: Bias in Private AI Development 7
      Example: Amazon's AI Hiring Tool 8
   The Role of Shareholders and Company Influence 8
      Analysis: Shareholder Pressure on AI Development 8
      Solution: Open-Source AI as a Counterbalance 8
   How Open-Sourcing Mitigates Bias 9
      Argument: Fostering Diversity in AI Development 9
      Example: Hugging Face and Community Contributions 9
Chapter 2: Public Monitoring of AI Development 10
   The Importance of Public Oversight 10
      Argument: Public Scrutiny as a Safeguard Against Ethical Flaws 10
      Example: The Cambridge Analytica Scandal 11
   Creating Mechanisms for Public Monitoring 11
      Discussion: Methods for Enabling Effective Public Oversight 11
      Solution: Open-Sourcing as a Framework for Public Monitoring 12
   Case Studies of Misuse or Fundamental Errors 12
      Analysis: Closed AI Systems and Ethical Breaches 12
      Example: Open-Source AI Uncovering Ethical Issues 12
Chapter 3: Governmental Adaptation and AI 14
   Governments Lagging Behind Technological Advances 14
      Argument: The Slow Pace of Government Response to AI 14
      Example: Legislative Delays in Autonomous Vehicles and Social Media 15
   Open-Source AI as a Tool for Government Oversight 15
      Argument: Leveraging Open-Source AI for Proactive Regulation 15
      Example: Government Collaboration with Open-Source AI Projects 16
   Proactive Lawmaking with AI Transparency 16
      Recommendation: Incentivizing Open-Source AI Development 16
      Example: Open-Source AI in Healthcare and Finance 17
Chapter 4: Ethics in AI Development 18
   The Need for Independent Ethical Oversight 18
      Argument: Lack of Independence in Corporate AI Ethics Boards 18
      Example: Google's AI Ethics Board Controversy 19

How Open-Source AI Ensures Ethical Development...19
    Argument: Open-Source AI Enables Global Ethical Auditing 19
    Solution: Partnerships Between Ethics Boards and the Open-Source Community 20
Case Studies of Ethical Failures and How Open-Sourcing Could Help..20
    Analysis: Failures in Closed AI Systems..20
    Example: How Open-Source Auditing Could Have Prevented Ethical Failures.......................................21

Chapter 5: Case Studies and Metrics **22**
Open-Source AI Success Stories 22
    Examples: Hugging Face and OpenAI...22
    Metrics: Diversity of Contributors and Community Engagement 23
Closed AI Failures...23
    Examples: Proprietary AI Systems and Their Pitfalls..23
    Metrics: Bias Reports, Security Breaches, and Lack of Oversight...24
Economic and Societal Impact of Open-Sourcing AI 24
    Analysis: Cost Savings, Societal Trust, and Sustainable Innovation 24

Chapter 6: The Future of AI Development **26**
Global Collaboration Through Open-Source AI 26
    Argument: Open-Source AI as a Global Ecosystem...26
    Example: Cross-Border Initiatives in Climate Change Modeling 27
Policy Recommendations for Open-Source AI 27
    Proposal: Government Policies to Promote Open-Source Development 27
    Example: The EU AI Act and Its Role in Promoting Transparency...28
Shaping the Future of AI Through Collaboration and Policy..28

Conclusion **30**
Summary of Key Arguments..30
Final Thoughts on the Future of AI 31
Call to Action..31

Personal Introduction: Why This eBook Was Created

As artificial intelligence (AI) becomes an increasingly integral part of our lives, shaping everything from how we interact with technology to how decisions are made in fields like healthcare, finance, and law, I felt it was crucial to engage in a meaningful conversation about the future of AI development. This eBook was born out of the desire to explore a critical question: How can we ensure that AI technologies are developed in a way that benefits everyone, rather than concentrating power in the hands of a few?

The answer, I believe in part, lies in open-source AI. I have created this eBook because I believe we recognize the immense potential that open-source development holds for fostering a more transparent, ethical, and collaborative approach to AI. Open-source AI provides a pathway toward building systems that are not only cutting-edge but also fair and accountable to the public. It invites participation from a diverse range of voices—researchers, developers, policymakers, and citizens—creating an ecosystem where innovation thrives and where ethical concerns are addressed openly and transparently.

At its core, this eBook is about advocating for the democratization of AI development. AI has the power to transform industries and solve some of the world's biggest challenges, but without public scrutiny and accountability, it also has the potential to exacerbate inequalities and entrench corporate control over vital technologies. By embracing open-source AI, we can ensure that the benefits of AI are shared more equitably, that its development remains transparent, and that it serves the broader public interest rather than narrow, profit-driven goals.

I would like the public to understand that open-source development of AI is not just about technology—it's about shaping the future of society. When AI systems are developed in the open, with contributions from around the world, we are more likely to create technologies that reflect our shared values of fairness, transparency, and inclusion. Open-source AI allows us to continually monitor and improve these systems, ensuring that they do not perpetuate harmful biases or lead to unethical outcomes.

This eBook is an invitation for everyone—whether you're a developer, a policymaker, or simply someone interested in the future of technology—to engage with the open-source movement. The choices we make today about how AI is developed will have long-lasting effects on society, and I believe that open-source AI represents the best path forward for creating a future where technology works for all of us, not just a select few.

By embracing open-source AI, we can help shape a world where AI is not a force for division or inequality, but a tool for collective progress, driven by collaboration, transparency, and a commitment to ethical innovation.

Introduction

Artificial Intelligence (AI) has become an integral part of modern life, shaping how individuals, businesses, and governments operate across various sectors. From self-driving cars to virtual assistants and personalized healthcare solutions, AI's influence continues to expand. While the potential of AI to drive innovation is undeniable, its development and deployment raise critical questions regarding ethics, transparency, and public oversight. In this book, we explore the role of open-source AI as a solution to these challenges, ensuring that AI technologies are developed in ways that are transparent, unbiased, and ethical.

Overview of AI's Role in Society

Brief History of AI

The development of AI dates back to the mid-20th century, when researchers first began exploring the possibility of creating machines that could simulate human intelligence. In 1956, the term "Artificial Intelligence" was coined during the Dartmouth Conference, marking the beginning of formal AI research. Early AI models focused on symbolic reasoning and problem-solving tasks, often based on manually coded algorithms. These systems laid the groundwork for modern AI, but they were limited by the computational power available at the time.

In the 1980s and 1990s, AI saw the rise of neural networks—mathematical models inspired by the structure of the human brain. Neural networks enabled computers to learn patterns from data rather than relying on explicit programming. One of the most famous early examples is the development of the backpropagation algorithm, which became a fundamental technique in training neural networks. However, progress was slow until the early 2000s, when advances in computing power, access to large datasets, and improvements in algorithms led to the AI revolution we see today.

By the 2010s, AI had moved beyond academic research into widespread commercial applications. Sectors like healthcare, finance, and robotics have benefited immensely from AI technologies. In healthcare, AI systems are now used to assist in diagnosing diseases, predicting patient outcomes, and personalizing treatment plans. For instance, AI models have significantly improved the accuracy of medical imaging analysis, helping doctors detect conditions like cancer at earlier stages.

In finance, AI-driven algorithms power automated trading systems, predicting market trends in milliseconds and executing trades without human intervention. These systems have transformed how financial institutions operate, increasing efficiency and profitability while reducing human error.

Robotics and automation have also been revolutionized by AI. Self-driving cars, powered by AI systems, are being tested on roads around the world, promising a future where autonomous vehicles reduce traffic accidents and improve transportation efficiency. Similarly, AI-driven robots are used in manufacturing to handle complex tasks with precision and speed, improving productivity in industries ranging from automotive to electronics.

Despite these advances, AI has introduced new challenges, particularly in terms of ethical dilemmas and the potential for bias. As AI's influence grows, so does the need for responsible development that prioritizes transparency and fairness. This is where open-source AI emerges as a critical solution.

Definition of Open-Source AI

Explanation of Open-Source AI

Open-source AI refers to artificial intelligence software and models whose source code is made freely available to the public. Unlike proprietary AI systems, which are developed and owned by private companies, open-source AI allows developers from around the world to access, modify, and contribute to the codebase. This collaborative model accelerates innovation by enabling a diverse group of contributors to share insights, solve problems, and improve the system in real-time.

The concept of open-source software is not new—it has been a cornerstone of technological innovation for decades. Open-source projects like Linux, the Apache web server, and MySQL databases have played pivotal roles in the growth of the internet and digital infrastructure. In recent years, AI has followed a similar path, with companies, research institutions, and independent developers embracing the open-source model.

Two prominent examples of open-source AI platforms are TensorFlow and Hugging Face. TensorFlow, developed by Google, is one of the most widely used open-source machine learning libraries. Released in 2015, TensorFlow provides tools for building and deploying AI models, from simple linear regression to complex deep neural networks. Its open-source nature has led to widespread adoption across industries, enabling developers to create cutting-edge AI applications, from natural language processing to computer vision. Google's decision to open-source TensorFlow was a turning point, allowing developers from all backgrounds to collaborate and innovate beyond what proprietary systems could achieve.

Hugging Face, another example, is an open-source platform specializing in natural language processing (NLP). It provides tools and models for tasks such as text generation, translation, and sentiment analysis. Hugging Face's community-driven model encourages collaboration among researchers, engineers, and data scientists, resulting in rapid innovation in the NLP field. Through its open-source ecosystem, Hugging Face has become a critical resource for companies, governments, and academic institutions looking to develop more advanced language-based AI systems.

Open-source AI democratizes access to advanced technologies, breaking down the barriers that typically prevent smaller organizations and individuals from leveraging the full potential of AI. By making code publicly available, open-source AI encourages transparency and fosters trust among users, developers, and the general public. In contrast, proprietary AI systems often operate as "black boxes," where the internal workings of the model are hidden from public scrutiny, raising concerns about bias, ethical practices, and the potential for misuse.

Thesis Statement

The argument presented in this book is that AI should be open-sourced to ensure transparency, prevent ethical mishaps, and reduce biases that are often embedded in privately developed models. When AI is developed in closed environments, the public has no way of understanding how decisions are made or whether those decisions are being influenced by biased data or the personal interests of the developers and companies involved.

In a world where AI is increasingly used to make critical decisions—such as hiring, loan approvals, and criminal sentencing—the potential for harm caused by biased or unethical AI systems is significant. Proprietary AI systems, which are designed and controlled by private corporations, are often driven by financial motives, with little regard for fairness or accountability. This leads to the risk of biased models that perpetuate inequality or make decisions that prioritize profits over ethical considerations.

Open-source AI offers a solution to these concerns by promoting transparency and enabling a wider community of developers, ethicists, and researchers to scrutinize and improve AI systems. By making the source code available for public review, open-source AI allows for independent audits, ensuring that biases can be identified and corrected before they cause harm. Additionally, the collaborative nature of open-source development encourages diverse perspectives, which can help prevent the formation of biased algorithms in the first place.

Scope and Objectives

This book will explore four key themes that highlight the importance of open-source AI in ensuring responsible AI development:

1. **Corporate Bias**: Proprietary AI systems often reflect the biases of the companies that develop them. This section will discuss how open-source AI can help mitigate corporate bias by encouraging more diverse contributions and independent oversight.
2. **Public Oversight**: Open-source AI provides a framework for public monitoring, enabling communities to scrutinize AI systems and flag potential ethical concerns. This section will explore mechanisms for ensuring public oversight in AI development.
3. **Government Lag**: Governments often struggle to keep pace with rapid technological advancements, particularly in the field of AI. This section will argue that open-source AI can help policymakers stay informed about emerging trends, allowing them to create proactive regulations.
4. **Ethical Safeguards**: AI systems must adhere to ethical standards to avoid causing harm. This section will examine how open-source AI promotes ethical development by encouraging transparency and allowing for independent audits.

These themes will frame the discussions throughout the book, offering a comprehensive view of why open-source AI is essential for creating a more transparent, ethical, and equitable technological future.

Chapter 1: AI Bias and Corporate Influence

Artificial intelligence is rapidly transforming industries by streamlining operations, making decisions based on data, and offering insights that humans may overlook. However, the use of AI by private corporations raises serious concerns about bias. Private AI systems, often developed behind closed doors and driven by profit motives, have been shown to perpetuate and even amplify existing biases in society. This section explores how corporate influence shapes AI development, the impact of biases in private AI systems, and how open-source AI offers a solution by fostering transparency and fairness.

Private AI and the Problem of Bias

Argument: Bias in Private AI Development

AI systems, particularly those developed by private companies, are not immune to the biases inherent in the data used to train them. These biases, whether explicit or implicit, can have far-reaching consequences. Private companies, motivated by profit, often prioritize efficiency and cost-effectiveness over ethical considerations, leading to the development of AI systems that may perpetuate societal inequalities. One of the most glaring examples of this is the racial bias found in facial recognition systems and the gender bias present in hiring algorithms.

Facial recognition technology has come under intense scrutiny due to its tendency to misidentify individuals from certain racial or ethnic groups. Studies have shown that AI systems used by law enforcement agencies or private security firms are more likely to misidentify people of color than white individuals. This bias has led to wrongful arrests and has sparked widespread concerns about the use of AI in policing and surveillance. When private companies develop such systems without sufficient oversight or transparency, the potential for harm is magnified.

Another area where bias has been evident is in AI-powered hiring tools. A notorious example is Amazon's AI hiring tool, which was designed to automate the screening of job applicants. The tool was meant to save time and identify the best candidates based on resumes submitted over a 10-year period. However, the system quickly demonstrated a significant bias against female candidates. Because the training data reflected the male-dominated tech industry, the AI inadvertently penalized resumes that contained words associated with women, such as "women's chess club captain." As a result, the AI favored male candidates, perpetuating the very gender bias that the technology was supposed to eliminate.

This case highlights how biased data used in AI systems can lead to discriminatory outcomes, often with serious consequences. Despite identifying the problem, Amazon ultimately abandoned the project, underscoring the difficulty of correcting bias once it has been deeply ingrained in an AI system. Such examples demonstrate that private companies, left to their own devices, may fail to address bias adequately—especially when addressing these issues conflicts with business interests.

Example: Amazon's AI Hiring Tool

Amazon's AI hiring tool serves as a clear illustration of the problem of bias in private AI systems. Developed to streamline hiring processes, the tool relied on historical data that reflected the predominantly male workforce in the tech industry. Since AI learns from the patterns in its training data, it perpetuated gender bias by ranking male candidates higher than equally qualified female candidates. The bias was not due to an explicit design flaw but rather an unintended consequence of using biased data. Amazon's inability to correct this bias before scrapping the project highlights the complexities of mitigating bias in proprietary AI systems developed by private corporations.

The Role of Shareholders and Company Influence

Analysis: Shareholder Pressure on AI Development

Corporate AI development is often driven by shareholder expectations and the pursuit of profit, which can have a significant impact on the ethical decisions surrounding AI. Shareholders in large tech companies are primarily concerned with financial returns, and this pressure can lead to decisions that prioritize short-term gains over long-term ethical considerations. For instance, companies may rush to deploy AI systems to the market without conducting thorough bias assessments or ethical reviews, especially if doing so would delay the product's release and impact revenue.

When profit is the driving force behind AI development, ethical concerns are often sidelined. Shareholders may push companies to adopt AI solutions that reduce costs, improve efficiency, or generate new revenue streams, but these systems may be inherently biased or lack transparency. The desire to remain competitive in a rapidly advancing technological landscape can lead companies to cut corners in terms of ethical oversight, resulting in AI systems that are not properly vetted for fairness or accountability.

For example, in the race to dominate the facial recognition market, some companies have prioritized speed and market penetration over addressing well-documented racial biases in their algorithms. This can lead to widespread adoption of biased systems before regulators or the public can assess their impacts, allowing corporate interests to take precedence over public welfare. As companies scale up their AI technologies, the potential for systemic bias grows, affecting millions of users or consumers.

Solution: Open-Source AI as a Counterbalance

Open-source AI offers a viable solution to the influence of shareholder pressure on AI development. By making the source code available to the public, open-source AI allows for independent contributions and scrutiny, reducing the risk that a single company or group of shareholders can dictate the ethical framework of the AI system. This collaborative model promotes fairness and inclusivity by encouraging a diverse array of contributors—ranging from academic researchers to independent developers and non-profit organizations—to participate in the development process.

Since open-source AI is not owned or controlled by a single entity, it is less likely to be driven solely by profit motives. Developers working on open-source AI projects are often motivated by ethical considerations, scientific curiosity, or a desire to solve complex problems, rather than the demands of shareholders. This diversity of motivations can help ensure that AI systems are designed with fairness and transparency in mind, rather than purely financial objectives. Moreover, the transparency inherent in open-source AI allows for continuous auditing and improvement, as independent contributors can identify and address biases that may have been overlooked by the original developers.

How Open-Sourcing Mitigates Bias

Argument: Fostering Diversity in AI Development

One of the key advantages of open-source AI is its ability to foster diversity in both the development process and the application of AI systems. In proprietary AI development, a small, often homogenous team of engineers typically controls the design, training, and deployment of AI systems. This limited perspective can lead to blind spots and biases that go unnoticed until the AI is deployed in real-world scenarios. In contrast, open-source AI invites contributions from a global pool of developers with varied backgrounds, experiences, and perspectives, reducing the likelihood that a single bias will dominate the system.

By encouraging a wider range of voices in AI development, open-source projects can mitigate the biases that arise from homogeneous teams. Contributors from different cultural, social, and professional backgrounds bring unique insights to the development process, identifying potential biases that might otherwise be overlooked. This collaborative approach ensures that the AI systems developed through open-source initiatives are more likely to reflect the diversity of the societies in which they are deployed, leading to fairer outcomes.

Example: Hugging Face and Community Contributions

A notable example of open-source AI successfully reducing bias is Hugging Face, a platform that specializes in natural language processing (NLP). Hugging Face has grown into a community-driven project, with contributions from thousands of developers worldwide. The platform allows researchers, engineers, and data scientists to collaborate on creating state-of-the-art language models that are freely available for public use.

One of the key benefits of Hugging Face's open-source approach is the transparency it provides. Because the models and code are publicly available, independent researchers and developers can audit the system for biases, suggest improvements, and contribute to a more equitable development process. This community-driven oversight helps prevent the kind of entrenched bias seen in proprietary systems. For instance, if an NLP model is found to exhibit gender or racial bias in its outputs, contributors can flag the issue, propose solutions, and submit code changes to address the bias. Hugging Face's open-source model fosters continuous improvements, driven by a global community committed to fairness and transparency.

Through projects like Hugging Face, open-source AI demonstrates how transparency and collaboration can reduce bias and lead to better, fairer outcomes. The ability to continuously audit and improve AI systems in an open environment helps ensure that AI technologies serve the broader public interest, rather than reinforcing existing societal inequalities.

Chapter 2: Public Monitoring of AI Development

As artificial intelligence becomes more pervasive in society, the need for effective public oversight becomes increasingly critical. AI systems are now used to make decisions that affect everything from consumer behavior to law enforcement, often without sufficient transparency. While the potential for AI to improve efficiency and decision-making is clear, its use also poses ethical risks—ranging from privacy violations to discrimination—if left unchecked. This section argues that public monitoring is essential to ensure the ethical development of AI and explores how open-source AI provides a framework for transparency and accountability.

The Importance of Public Oversight

Argument: Public Scrutiny as a Safeguard Against Ethical Flaws

AI technologies, especially when developed and deployed by private companies or governments, can operate as "black boxes"—complex systems whose inner workings are hidden from public view. Without transparency, it becomes nearly impossible to scrutinize AI decisions, making it difficult to detect ethical breaches or unintended biases until real harm is done. Public oversight, however, offers a vital mechanism to ensure that AI systems are used responsibly and ethically. When AI development is transparent and subject to public scrutiny, ethical flaws and misuses of the technology can be identified and addressed before they cause significant damage.

One of the clearest examples of the dangers of unchecked AI development is the **Cambridge Analytica scandal**, which exposed the ethical pitfalls of using AI and big data without adequate oversight. In 2018, it was revealed that Cambridge Analytica, a political consulting firm, had improperly harvested the personal data of millions of Facebook users without their consent. This data was then used to build detailed psychological profiles that allowed the company to target individuals with highly personalized political advertisements during the 2016 U.S. presidential election and the Brexit referendum.

The scandal highlighted how AI algorithms, when combined with large datasets, can be used for political manipulation. The algorithms developed by Cambridge Analytica were designed to influence voter behavior by predicting and targeting users with specific content based on their online behavior. While the company claimed to offer cutting-edge data analytics, the lack of transparency around how their AI systems functioned and the unethical use of personal data raised significant concerns. If these AI tools had been subject to public oversight or open-source scrutiny, the ethical breaches—such as the violation of privacy and manipulation of voters—could have been flagged earlier, preventing widespread misuse of AI for political purposes.

Public oversight can act as a counterbalance to the profit-driven motives of private companies and the secretive nature of governmental AI systems. It allows for independent audits and public discourse on how AI is being used, ensuring that systems are held accountable to societal standards of ethics and fairness. Open-source AI provides the perfect environment for such scrutiny by allowing anyone to access, examine, and challenge AI systems, leading to greater accountability.

Example: The Cambridge Analytica Scandal

The Cambridge Analytica case underscores the risks of developing and using AI in closed environments without public oversight. If the algorithms used by the company had been developed within an open-source framework, where the public or independent watchdogs could have scrutinized the AI's inner workings, the ethical violations may have been detected early. Public scrutiny would have raised red flags about how personal data was being collected and used for political purposes, potentially preventing the abuse of AI for voter manipulation.

Creating Mechanisms for Public Monitoring

Discussion: Methods for Enabling Effective Public Oversight

To ensure that AI systems are developed and used ethically, it is critical to create mechanisms for public monitoring. Transparency in AI development not only fosters trust but also empowers a wider audience to engage in ethical discourse and oversight. There are several practical methods to enable public monitoring of AI systems, with open-source platforms serving as the most promising solution.

One effective method is the publication of AI code in **open repositories**. When the source code of an AI system is made publicly available, it allows developers, researchers, and the general public to inspect the underlying algorithms and identify potential issues, such as bias or unethical behavior. Open repositories like GitHub enable developers to share their code with the broader community, inviting contributions, improvements, and audits. This openness ensures that the development process is transparent and accessible, allowing for real-time monitoring by a diverse range of stakeholders.

Another key mechanism for public monitoring is the implementation of **transparent auditing processes**. Independent audits of AI systems—conducted by third-party organizations, academia, or non-profit watchdogs—can help verify that AI technologies comply with ethical standards and legal regulations. These audits should be conducted regularly, particularly in sectors where AI systems make decisions that directly affect individuals, such as criminal justice, healthcare, and finance. Public reports on these audits should be made available to ensure transparency and accountability.

For instance, **transparent audit processes** can be applied to facial recognition systems used by law enforcement agencies. By conducting regular audits and making the results publicly available, these agencies can demonstrate that their AI systems are not being misused for mass surveillance or unfair profiling based on race or ethnicity. Public audits also allow for corrective action if ethical violations are identified, providing a safeguard against the misuse of AI technologies in sensitive areas.

The **open-source model** provides a natural platform for real-time monitoring and ethical review. Open-source AI enables developers to continually refine and improve systems, with a global community of contributors who can identify risks and ethical concerns as they arise. Because the development process is transparent, any potential issues, such as discriminatory algorithms or breaches of privacy, can be addressed before they have widespread consequences. Open-source AI encourages the kind of collaboration and public engagement that ensures AI systems are held accountable to ethical standards.

Solution: Open-Sourcing as a Framework for Public Monitoring

Open-source AI creates a built-in framework for public monitoring by making both the development process and the final product accessible to the public. This level of transparency allows for real-time oversight by a broad range of stakeholders, including researchers, developers, and civil society organizations. When AI systems are developed in an open-source environment, it becomes much harder for ethical breaches to go unnoticed, as the global community can continuously audit and improve the technology. This transparency is essential for ensuring that AI systems are used responsibly and in ways that serve the public good.

Case Studies of Misuse or Fundamental Errors

Analysis: Closed AI Systems and Ethical Breaches

The potential for ethical violations is significantly higher when AI systems are developed in closed, proprietary environments. In such cases, the lack of transparency means that there is no public oversight to catch ethical errors, and harmful practices can go unchecked until it is too late. Two prominent examples of ethical breaches in closed AI systems include the misuse of surveillance technologies in China and discriminatory algorithms used in the criminal justice system.

In China, the government has deployed AI-powered surveillance systems to monitor and control the population, particularly targeting minority groups such as the Uighurs. These systems use facial recognition and other AI tools to track individuals' movements and activities, creating a surveillance state that has been widely criticized for human rights abuses. The AI systems employed in these surveillance programs are highly secretive, with little information available to the public about how they operate or the ethical considerations behind their use. Without public oversight, these AI systems have enabled the widespread violation of privacy and human rights, demonstrating the dangers of closed AI development.

Similarly, AI algorithms used in the U.S. criminal justice system have faced criticism for perpetuating racial bias. Predictive policing tools, for example, analyze historical crime data to forecast where crimes are likely to occur and who is likely to commit them. These algorithms are often trained on biased data, leading to disproportionately high policing in minority communities. Because these AI systems are proprietary, the public and independent researchers have limited access to the algorithms and data, making it difficult to assess the full extent of the bias. As a result, these systems continue to contribute to racial disparities in policing and incarceration rates.

Example: Open-Source AI Uncovering Ethical Issues

In contrast to the examples of misuse in closed AI systems, open-source development has helped uncover and address ethical concerns early on, preventing broader societal harm. A key example is the open-source community's role in identifying and correcting biases in natural language processing (NLP) models. NLP models, such as those used in chatbots and virtual assistants, often develop gender or racial biases based on the data they are trained on. In one high-profile case, the open-source community flagged bias in a popular NLP model that associated gender-specific terms with certain professions—e.g., "doctor" with "he" and "nurse" with "she."

By examining the publicly available source code and training data, independent researchers were able to identify the bias and propose modifications to correct it. This collaborative effort led to a more equitable model that did not reinforce harmful stereotypes. The ability of the open-source community to detect and correct ethical issues before they become ingrained in widely used AI systems demonstrates the power of public monitoring in ensuring responsible AI development.

In addition, open-source AI models have been instrumental in the field of healthcare, where transparency is crucial for ensuring that AI-driven medical decisions are accurate and fair. For instance, open-source projects that analyze medical imaging data have benefited from the scrutiny of medical experts and AI researchers, who work together to improve the accuracy and fairness of diagnostic algorithms. This collaborative approach has led to more robust and ethical AI tools in healthcare, preventing the kind of biased decision-making that could otherwise lead to misdiagnosis or unequal access to treatment.

Chapter 3: Governmental Adaptation and AI

The rapid development of artificial intelligence has left governments around the world struggling to keep pace with technological advancements. While AI has the potential to revolutionize industries such as healthcare, finance, and transportation, the speed at which AI technologies evolve often outpaces the creation of laws and regulations necessary to govern their use. This delay can result in significant societal harm, as policymakers scramble to address issues that have already caused widespread consequences. In this section, we will explore how governments lag behind in adapting to AI, the potential of open-source AI to provide critical insights for proactive regulation, and how lawmakers can encourage AI transparency and ethical development.

Governments Lagging Behind Technological Advances

Argument: The Slow Pace of Government Response to AI

One of the most significant challenges in regulating artificial intelligence is the sheer speed of technological advancements. AI systems are continuously evolving, and new applications emerge far faster than the legislative process can accommodate. Governments, with their bureaucratic processes and extended timelines for drafting and passing laws, often find themselves in a reactive position, attempting to address AI-related issues only after they have caused harm. This lag in governmental adaptation has been evident in several key areas, where the absence of timely regulation has allowed ethical and safety concerns to escalate unchecked.

A clear example of this can be seen in the regulation of **autonomous vehicles**. Self-driving cars, once considered a futuristic technology, have already become a reality, with companies like Tesla, Waymo, and Uber testing autonomous vehicles on public roads. However, despite the rapid development and deployment of these technologies, governments have been slow to establish comprehensive regulations governing their use. The lack of clear rules regarding the safety standards, liability in the event of accidents, and the ethical programming of these vehicles has created confusion among manufacturers, regulators, and the public.

In 2018, a pedestrian was killed by a self-driving Uber vehicle in Arizona, sparking widespread concerns about the safety of autonomous cars. The incident highlighted the absence of robust safety regulations and the failure of lawmakers to foresee and address the ethical implications of AI-powered vehicles. The delay in creating legislation for autonomous vehicles has led to a patchwork of state-by-state regulations in the United States, with little consistency or oversight at the federal level. This regulatory vacuum has not only endangered public safety but has also slowed down the broader adoption of self-driving technology due to uncertainty over legal responsibilities.

Another area where governments have lagged behind is the regulation of **social media content moderation**. The rise of AI-driven algorithms to manage online content has significantly altered how information is disseminated, but lawmakers have struggled to keep pace with the technology's implications for free speech, privacy, and the spread of misinformation. Social media platforms like Facebook, Twitter, and YouTube use AI to automatically flag and remove harmful content, but these systems have frequently been criticized for both under-censoring and over-censoring content. In many cases, harmful misinformation—such as during election campaigns or the COVID-19 pandemic—has spread unchecked because AI moderation systems failed to catch it in time. On the other hand, legitimate content has been mistakenly removed, raising concerns about the accuracy and fairness of AI moderation.

These examples demonstrate that without timely and effective regulations, AI technologies can exacerbate existing social problems or create new ethical dilemmas. Governments must move beyond a reactive stance and adopt a more proactive approach to AI regulation if they are to safeguard public welfare and maintain control over rapidly advancing technologies.

Example: Legislative Delays in Autonomous Vehicles and Social Media

The failure of governments to regulate autonomous vehicles and social media content moderation in a timely manner illustrates the broader issue of governmental lag in addressing AI developments. In both cases, the absence of clear, proactive regulation has allowed AI technologies to be deployed without sufficient oversight, leading to significant societal harm. If lawmakers continue to lag behind AI innovation, similar issues will arise in other sectors, such as healthcare and finance, where the ethical use of AI is critical.

Open-Source AI as a Tool for Government Oversight

Argument: Leveraging Open-Source AI for Proactive Regulation

While governments may struggle to keep pace with AI developments, open-source AI offers a valuable tool for addressing this challenge. By leveraging open-source AI platforms, lawmakers and regulators can gain early insights into emerging AI trends and technological advancements, allowing them to draft legislation that is both timely and effective. Open-source AI provides a transparent and accessible environment in which governments can observe how AI systems are being developed and deployed, enabling them to identify potential ethical issues and regulatory gaps before they cause harm.

One of the key benefits of open-source AI is the **collaborative nature** of its development. Because open-source AI systems are developed in public forums, anyone—including policymakers, ethicists, and regulators—can access the code and contribute to its improvement. This transparency allows lawmakers to monitor ongoing AI projects, assess their potential societal impacts, and collaborate with the AI community to ensure that ethical considerations are incorporated from the outset. In contrast, proprietary AI systems are typically developed behind closed doors, making it difficult for regulators to gain the information they need to craft effective policies.

For example, **collaboration between governments and open-source AI projects** could help policymakers stay ahead of developments in areas like **data privacy**. AI systems that process large amounts of personal data, such as those used in healthcare or finance, pose significant privacy risks if not properly regulated. By working with open-source AI projects, governments can better understand how data is being collected, stored, and analyzed, and they can ensure that data privacy regulations keep pace with technological innovations. Open-source AI platforms, such as TensorFlow or OpenAI's early models, provide a transparent foundation upon which governments can build regulatory frameworks that protect individual privacy while fostering innovation.

Moreover, governments can use open-source AI to **develop regulatory tools** of their own. By creating and deploying open-source AI models designed to detect unethical AI practices or identify algorithmic bias, regulators can take a proactive stance in monitoring AI applications across different industries. These regulatory AI tools can be continuously updated and improved by the open-source community, ensuring that they remain effective in a rapidly evolving technological landscape.

Example: Government Collaboration with Open-Source AI Projects

Collaboration between governments and open-source AI projects has already shown promise in addressing issues like data privacy and algorithmic fairness. For instance, the

European Union's General Data Protection Regulation (GDPR) has influenced the development of AI systems that comply with stringent data privacy standards. By engaging with the open-source AI community, the EU has been able to ensure that AI systems developed within its jurisdiction prioritize privacy and transparency. Similar collaborations in other regions and industries could help ensure that governments remain proactive in regulating AI technologies.

Proactive Lawmaking with AI Transparency

Recommendation: Incentivizing Open-Source AI Development

To ensure that governments can effectively regulate AI technologies, it is essential to encourage the development of **open-source AI** models that promote transparency, particularly in regulated industries such as healthcare and finance. AI systems used in these sectors often make decisions that have profound implications for individuals and society, such as determining access to medical treatments or approving loans. In these high-stakes environments, the need for transparency is especially critical to ensure that AI decisions are fair, accountable, and free from bias.

One way governments can incentivize the development of open-source AI is by offering **funding** and **tax incentives** to organizations and developers who create transparent AI models. Governments could establish grants or subsidies for AI projects that commit to making their code publicly available and adhere to ethical standards. By providing financial support for open-source AI development, governments can encourage the creation of AI systems that are accessible for public scrutiny and contribute to the broader goal of ethical AI.

In addition to financial incentives, governments can introduce **regulatory requirements** that mandate the use of open-source AI in certain industries. For example, in the healthcare sector, where patient outcomes depend on accurate and unbiased AI-driven diagnostics, regulators could require that AI models used in medical devices be open-source, allowing independent experts to audit the code and ensure that it complies with ethical guidelines. Similarly, in the financial industry, where AI is used to make lending or investment decisions, open-source requirements could help prevent discriminatory algorithms that disadvantage certain groups of people.

By promoting open-source AI, governments can not only improve transparency but also foster a more competitive and innovative AI ecosystem. When AI models are open-source, smaller companies and startups have the opportunity to build on existing technology rather than having to develop proprietary systems from scratch. This can lead to faster innovation, as developers can collaborate and share knowledge freely, while also ensuring that AI systems remain accountable to the public.

Example: Open-Source AI in Healthcare and Finance

In industries like healthcare and finance, where transparency and fairness are paramount, open-source AI can play a crucial role in ensuring ethical outcomes. For instance, AI systems used to analyze medical imaging data or predict patient outcomes must be transparent to allow for independent validation of their accuracy and fairness. By mandating the use of open-source AI in these critical areas, governments can ensure that AI systems adhere to the highest ethical standards, while also encouraging innovation through collaboration.

Chapter 4: Ethics in AI Development

As artificial intelligence becomes increasingly integrated into critical decision-making processes—ranging from healthcare to criminal justice—the need for ethical AI development is more urgent than ever. AI systems, which often operate with minimal human oversight, have the potential to produce biased, unfair, or harmful outcomes if they are not developed with strong ethical safeguards in place. Unfortunately, many companies developing AI prioritize profit and competitive advantage over ethics, leading to decisions that can have serious societal repercussions. In this section, we explore the necessity of independent ethical oversight in AI development, how open-source AI can foster ethical accountability, and case studies of ethical failures that highlight the importance of transparency in AI.

The Need for Independent Ethical Oversight

Argument: Lack of Independence in Corporate AI Ethics Boards

One of the most significant challenges in AI development is the conflict of interest that arises when companies attempt to regulate themselves. Many organizations developing AI systems set up internal ethics boards to oversee AI development, but these boards often lack true independence and authority. In many cases, these boards are comprised of employees or advisors who are influenced by the company's financial interests, leading to ethical oversight that is compromised or ineffective. Without independent ethical oversight, companies are more likely to prioritize profit, speed to market, and competitive advantage over fairness, transparency, and accountability.

The case of **Google's AI ethics board controversy** in 2019 is a prime example of how internal ethical oversight can fail. In an effort to address growing concerns over the ethical implications of its AI projects, Google established an external advisory council called the Advanced Technology External Advisory Council (ATEAC). The council was tasked with providing guidance on ethical issues related to AI development, such as facial recognition and machine learning. However, the council's formation quickly became embroiled in controversy when it was revealed that several members had conflicts of interest and questionable qualifications to provide unbiased ethical advice.

One board member, for example, was the president of a conservative think tank that had been criticized for promoting anti-LGBTQ views, leading to a public outcry over her appointment. Another member was a representative from the defense industry, raising concerns about potential conflicts with AI ethics discussions related to military applications. The controversy highlighted the difficulty of establishing an independent ethical board that could effectively challenge Google's AI projects, many of which were being developed for lucrative markets. Within a week of its creation, Google dissolved the board, citing internal disagreements and public backlash.

The rapid dissolution of Google's ethics board underscores the limitations of corporate-led ethical oversight. When ethics boards are not truly independent, they lack the authority to challenge the company's decisions in a meaningful way. In many cases, such boards are established as a public relations measure, rather than as a serious mechanism for ensuring ethical AI development. Without independent oversight, companies are more likely to push forward with AI projects that may pose ethical risks, especially when those projects promise significant financial returns.

Example: Google's AI Ethics Board Controversy

Google's failed attempt to create an AI ethics board reveals the challenges of ensuring ethical oversight within corporate environments. The lack of independence, coupled with conflicting interests among board members, undermined the board's credibility and effectiveness. This case illustrates the need for more robust and independent mechanisms of ethical oversight, particularly in companies that are at the forefront of AI innovation.

How Open-Source AI Ensures Ethical Development

Argument: Open-Source AI Enables Global Ethical Auditing

Unlike closed AI systems developed by private companies, open-source AI offers a framework for ethical development that is inherently more transparent and accountable. One of the key benefits of open-source AI is that it allows for global, independent auditing by a diverse group of experts. When the source code for an AI system is made publicly available, ethicists, researchers, and developers from around the world can examine the system for potential ethical concerns, such as bias, discrimination, or privacy violations. This collaborative approach to ethical oversight ensures that a wide range of perspectives are considered, reducing the likelihood that harmful biases or ethical blind spots will go unnoticed.

Open-source systems also foster a culture of continuous ethical monitoring. Because the development process is open and collaborative, ethical issues can be flagged and addressed early in the development cycle. Global experts can contribute to the identification of risks, propose solutions, and implement improvements, creating a dynamic system of ethical checks and balances. This is especially important in AI development, where the potential for harm is high, and ethical issues are often difficult to predict in advance. By involving a global community of contributors, open-source AI ensures that ethical considerations are not an afterthought but are integrated into the development process from the start.

One way to strengthen ethical oversight in open-source AI is to **encourage partnerships between ethics boards and the open-source community**. Independent ethics boards, comprised of ethicists, technologists, and human rights advocates, can work alongside open-source developers to provide continuous ethical guidance. These boards would not be tied to any single company or financial interest, allowing them to operate with true independence. By collaborating with the open-source community, these boards can help ensure that AI systems are developed in accordance with broad ethical standards that prioritize human rights, fairness, and transparency.

Open-source AI can also help address one of the most significant ethical challenges in AI development: bias. Many AI systems are trained on datasets that reflect historical biases, leading to outcomes that disadvantage certain groups of people. Open-source projects allow developers to continuously audit training data and algorithms for bias, making it easier to identify and mitigate these issues before they cause harm. The ability to crowdsource ethical reviews of AI systems ensures that ethical concerns are addressed by a diverse group of stakeholders, rather than being left in the hands of a single company or development team.

Solution: Partnerships Between Ethics Boards and the Open-Source Community

To promote ethical AI development, governments, academic institutions, and non-profits should encourage the creation of independent ethics boards that collaborate with the open-source AI community. These partnerships would enable continuous ethical auditing and provide a mechanism for addressing ethical concerns as they arise. By involving a broad range of stakeholders in the development process, open-source AI ensures that ethical standards are maintained across industries and applications.

Case Studies of Ethical Failures and How Open-Sourcing Could Help

Analysis: Failures in Closed AI Systems

There are numerous examples of closed AI systems that have failed ethically, leading to significant harm. One of the most concerning areas where AI has failed is in **predictive policing algorithms**, which are used by law enforcement agencies to forecast where crimes are likely to occur and who is most likely to commit them. These algorithms, often developed in closed environments, are trained on historical crime data that disproportionately reflects policing practices in low-income and minority communities. As a result, predictive policing systems tend to reinforce existing racial biases, leading to over-policing of marginalized groups and perpetuating cycles of discrimination.

A well-known example is the **COMPAS algorithm**, which was used in the United States to assess the likelihood of criminal defendants reoffending. COMPAS scores were used by judges to inform sentencing decisions, with the idea that high-risk individuals should receive harsher penalties to prevent future crimes. However, an investigation by ProPublica revealed that the algorithm was biased against Black defendants, who were more likely to be incorrectly classified as high risk compared to white defendants. The proprietary nature of COMPAS made it difficult for independent researchers to audit the algorithm, and the bias in the system went undetected for years. The use of biased AI in the criminal justice system has had far-reaching consequences, exacerbating racial disparities in sentencing and incarceration rates.

If COMPAS had been developed as an open-source system, its bias could have been detected and addressed much earlier. Independent researchers and ethicists would have been able to audit the algorithm, identify the sources of bias in the training data, and propose modifications to ensure fairer outcomes. Open-source auditing allows for continuous improvement of AI systems, making it less likely that biased algorithms will be deployed without sufficient scrutiny.

Another area where closed AI systems have failed is in **facial recognition technology**. These systems have been widely criticized for their poor accuracy when identifying individuals from minority groups, particularly women of color. One high-profile case involved Amazon's **Rekognition** software, which was found to have significantly higher error rates when identifying Black and Asian faces compared to white faces. Despite these concerns, Rekognition was marketed to law enforcement agencies as a tool for identifying criminal suspects, raising serious ethical questions about its use in policing. The proprietary nature of the software made it difficult for independent researchers to audit or challenge its accuracy, and the lack of transparency around how the system was trained and tested allowed the bias to persist.

If facial recognition algorithms like Rekognition were open-source, they would be subject to much greater scrutiny. Researchers and developers from diverse backgrounds could audit the system for bias, test its accuracy across different demographic groups, and propose improvements. Open-source auditing would ensure that facial recognition systems are not deployed until they meet rigorous ethical and technical standards, reducing the risk of harm to marginalized communities.

Example: How Open-Source Auditing Could Have Prevented Ethical Failures

In both the COMPAS and Rekognition cases, the closed nature of the AI systems allowed significant ethical failures to go unchecked. Open-sourcing these systems could have provided a platform for independent researchers to audit the algorithms, identify biases, and propose solutions before the systems were widely deployed. By making AI systems transparent and accessible to a global community of experts, open-source AI offers a powerful tool for preventing ethical failures and ensuring that AI systems serve the public good.

Chapter 5: Case Studies and Metrics

The debate over open-source versus proprietary AI is more than a philosophical discussion about transparency and collaboration—it has real-world implications. Open-source AI has demonstrated significant success, particularly in promoting innovation, reducing bias, and fostering community-driven development. At the same time, proprietary AI systems have shown that a lack of oversight and transparency can lead to ethical failures, biases, and security risks. This section explores these dynamics through case studies of open-source AI success stories and proprietary AI failures, along with an analysis of how open-source AI has had a positive economic and societal impact.

Open-Source AI Success Stories

Examples: Hugging Face and OpenAI

Two notable success stories in the world of open-source AI are **Hugging Face** and **OpenAI** (during its early stages). Both platforms have become benchmarks for how open-source AI can drive innovation, reduce bias, and build strong community-driven ecosystems. These platforms illustrate the key strengths of open-source AI: transparency, collaboration, and the ability to harness diverse perspectives to improve AI systems continuously.

Hugging Face has revolutionized natural language processing (NLP) by offering an open-source platform for developers, researchers, and companies to access state-of-the-art machine learning models for tasks such as text classification, translation, and conversational AI. The platform's open-source approach has empowered thousands of contributors worldwide to build, share, and improve NLP models, driving significant advancements in language processing. Hugging Face's models, particularly those based on the **Transformers library**, have been widely adopted across industries, including healthcare, education, and finance, proving the viability of community-driven innovation.

The platform's commitment to transparency has also helped address bias in AI models. By making the code and models publicly available, Hugging Face allows researchers to audit these models for biases and other ethical concerns. For instance, users have flagged issues of gender and racial bias in text generation models, and the community has worked together to improve these models. This continuous auditing process is a key advantage of open-source AI, as it enables real-time improvements and ethical oversight that would be more difficult to achieve in proprietary settings.

Similarly, **OpenAI** began as an open-source AI research organization with the mission of ensuring that artificial general intelligence (AGI) would benefit all of humanity. OpenAI initially shared its research and code freely with the public, encouraging collaboration and knowledge-sharing across the global AI community. This openness fostered significant innovation, particularly in the development of the **GPT (Generative Pre-trained Transformer)** models, which have since become some of the most influential AI models for tasks such as language generation and understanding.

While OpenAI has since moved to a more closed model, its early open-source approach demonstrated the immense potential of collaborative AI development. During its open phase, OpenAI not only contributed to technical breakthroughs but also created a global community of researchers and developers who worked together to address ethical concerns, such as reducing bias in language models and ensuring that AI systems were used responsibly.

Metrics: Diversity of Contributors and Community Engagement

A key measure of success for open-source AI projects like Hugging Face and OpenAI is the **diversity of contributors** and the **level of community engagement**. Both platforms have attracted a wide range of contributors from different backgrounds, including academic researchers, industry professionals, and independent developers. This diversity is crucial for reducing bias in AI systems, as a more varied group of contributors brings different perspectives and experiences to the development process.

In terms of metrics, **Hugging Face's GitHub repository** has thousands of contributors, representing one of the largest and most active open-source AI communities. The number of forks, stars, and contributions on the platform is a strong indicator of community engagement and collaboration. Additionally, Hugging Face has prioritized inclusivity by creating tools that are accessible to both AI experts and those with less technical expertise, further broadening its user base and fostering a diverse community.

Similarly, during its early stages, **OpenAI's research papers and code repositories** were widely shared and cited by the academic community, reflecting its success in building an engaged, collaborative ecosystem. The open access to cutting-edge models like GPT also allowed for a wide range of applications across industries, further demonstrating the impact of open-source AI on innovation and societal progress.

Closed AI Failures

Examples: Proprietary AI Systems and Their Pitfalls

While open-source AI has demonstrated significant benefits, closed AI systems—those developed in secret by private companies—have often been plagued by ethical failures, bias, and security vulnerabilities. The lack of transparency in proprietary AI makes it difficult for independent researchers or the public to scrutinize these systems, which can lead to harmful outcomes.

One of the most notorious examples of a closed AI failure is the **COMPAS (Correctional Offender Management Profiling for Alternative Sanctions)** algorithm, a proprietary tool used in the U.S. criminal justice system to assess the risk of defendants reoffending. COMPAS was widely adopted by courts to inform decisions about bail and sentencing, but an investigation by **ProPublica** revealed that the algorithm was biased against Black defendants. Black defendants were more likely to be classified as high-risk compared to white defendants, even though they were no more likely to reoffend. The proprietary nature of COMPAS made it difficult for external experts to audit the system, and it took years for the bias to be exposed.

Another example is **Amazon's Rekognition**, a facial recognition system that was sold to law enforcement agencies despite widespread concerns about its accuracy and bias. Independent tests found that Rekognition performed poorly when identifying people of color, particularly Black women, but these findings were not publicized until civil society groups and researchers applied pressure for independent audits. The lack of transparency around Rekognition's development and deployment raised serious concerns about its use in policing, and Amazon eventually paused the sale of the technology to law enforcement following public backlash.

Metrics: Bias Reports, Security Breaches, and Lack of Oversight

The failures of closed AI systems can be measured through a variety of **metrics**, including reports of bias, security breaches, and a lack of regulatory oversight. For example, the

COMPAS algorithm faced significant criticism for perpetuating racial bias, with ProPublica's report providing detailed statistics on how often the algorithm misclassified defendants based on race. Similarly, Amazon's Rekognition was flagged by independent research groups for having **false-positive rates** that were disproportionately higher for minority groups, a key indicator of the system's unreliability and bias.

In addition to bias, closed AI systems are often vulnerable to **security breaches** due to their opaque development processes. For example, proprietary AI models used in industries like finance or healthcare have been targeted by hackers, and without public access to the code, it is difficult for external experts to assess the security vulnerabilities of these systems.

The **lack of regulatory oversight** is another key metric of failure in proprietary AI systems. In many cases, closed AI systems are deployed without proper audits or testing, which can result in ethical and legal issues. The absence of third-party reviews in systems like COMPAS and Rekognition highlights the dangers of deploying AI systems without sufficient checks on their fairness and accuracy.

Economic and Societal Impact of Open-Sourcing AI

Analysis: Cost Savings, Societal Trust, and Sustainable Innovation

One of the most compelling arguments for open-source AI is the positive **economic and societal impact** it generates. Open-source AI reduces development costs, fosters trust among users and stakeholders, and creates a sustainable environment for innovation that benefits society as a whole.

Cost savings are one of the most tangible benefits of open-source AI. For small companies, startups, or academic researchers, developing AI systems from scratch can be prohibitively expensive. Open-source AI platforms, like TensorFlow and Hugging Face, provide access to pre-built models and tools, allowing organizations to build on existing technology rather than starting from zero. This not only reduces development costs but also accelerates the deployment of AI applications in industries such as healthcare, education, and transportation.

For example, startups working on medical diagnostics can leverage open-source AI models to develop tools that assist doctors in identifying diseases like cancer or diabetes. By using open-source models, these companies can reduce the time and cost of bringing their products to market, making healthcare innovations more accessible to patients and providers.

Beyond economic savings, open-source AI fosters **societal trust**. When AI systems are transparent and open to public scrutiny, users are more likely to trust the technology and its outcomes. Trust is particularly important in sectors like healthcare and finance, where AI is used to make decisions that directly impact people's lives. Open-source AI allows patients, regulators, and other stakeholders to verify that AI systems are making fair, unbiased decisions, thus enhancing societal trust in AI technologies.

Finally, open-source AI promotes **sustainable innovation**. The collaborative nature of open-source projects ensures that AI development is not concentrated in the hands of a few large companies but is distributed across a global network of contributors. This decentralization allows for more diverse ideas, faster innovation, and the continuous improvement of AI systems. Open-source AI also helps prevent monopolistic control of AI technologies, fostering a more equitable and competitive landscape for AI development.

In conclusion, open-source AI has proven to be a powerful driver of innovation, bias reduction, and community engagement, as demonstrated by platforms like Hugging Face and the earlier phases of OpenAI. In contrast, proprietary AI systems have often failed ethically due to a lack of transparency and oversight, leading to biased outcomes and security vulnerabilities. The economic and societal benefits of open-source AI—such as cost savings, increased trust, and sustainable innovation—underscore the importance of promoting open-source development in the AI field. By embracing open-source principles, we can ensure that AI technologies are developed in ways that benefit society as a whole.

Chapter 6: The Future of AI Development

As artificial intelligence continues to evolve, its future development will be shaped not only by technological innovation but also by how well the global community addresses ethical, social, and political challenges. Open-source AI stands as a critical factor in this future, offering a collaborative framework that transcends national borders and empowers individuals and organizations worldwide to contribute to AI's growth. By encouraging open-source development, governments and international organizations can help create a more equitable, transparent, and innovative AI ecosystem that addresses global challenges and ensures that the benefits of AI are widely shared. In this section, we will explore the potential of global collaboration through open-source AI and outline policy recommendations that can foster a more inclusive and sustainable future for AI development.

Global Collaboration Through Open-Source AI

Argument: Open-Source AI as a Global Ecosystem

One of the most powerful advantages of open-source AI is its ability to foster a global ecosystem where collaboration transcends national borders. Unlike proprietary AI, which is often developed in isolation by private companies or within specific national jurisdictions, open-source AI invites contributions from developers, researchers, and institutions from around the world. This collaborative approach accelerates innovation by allowing people with diverse perspectives, skills, and expertise to work together on common challenges. It also ensures that AI solutions are not limited by the interests of a single company or country but are shaped by a collective effort to address global needs.

The international nature of open-source AI allows it to serve as a platform for solving some of the most pressing problems facing humanity today. Global challenges such as climate change, public health crises, and poverty require solutions that are not confined by borders, and open-source AI provides the necessary infrastructure for international collaboration. By pooling resources and knowledge across countries, open-source AI enables the development of solutions that are more comprehensive, scalable, and inclusive.

A prime example of how open-source AI has fostered global collaboration is in the area of **climate change modeling**. Climate change is a complex and multifaceted problem that requires vast amounts of data and computational power to understand and address. Open-source AI has played a crucial role in the development of advanced climate models, which are used to simulate the Earth's climate system and predict future environmental changes. These models rely on data from satellites, sensors, and climate monitoring stations around the world, making them truly global in scope.

Several open-source AI initiatives have emerged to tackle climate-related challenges. For instance, the **Climate Change AI** initiative brings together researchers, data scientists, and policymakers from different countries to explore how AI can be used to mitigate the impacts of climate change. Through open collaboration, this initiative has developed AI tools for predicting extreme weather events, optimizing renewable energy sources, and modeling carbon emissions. By making these tools and models freely available, the open-source community enables governments, non-profits, and researchers to access the latest technologies and apply them to local contexts, from monitoring deforestation in the Amazon to improving urban resilience against heat waves.

Another example of cross-border collaboration facilitated by open-source AI is the **AI for Good Global Summit**, which is organized by the International Telecommunication Union (ITU) and brings together AI experts from around the world to develop AI solutions for the United Nations' Sustainable Development Goals (SDGs). By leveraging open-source platforms, participants in the summit collaborate on projects such as improving healthcare delivery in low-income countries, addressing food insecurity, and enhancing disaster response efforts. These initiatives illustrate the potential of open-source AI to serve as a global catalyst for positive change, fostering international cooperation and addressing challenges that affect all of humanity.

Example: Cross-Border Initiatives in Climate Change Modeling

The use of open-source AI in climate change modeling is a testament to how international collaboration can produce innovative solutions to global problems. Projects like **Climate Change AI** leverage the collective intelligence of researchers across multiple countries, developing tools that can predict and mitigate the impacts of climate change. These tools are shared freely, allowing countries with limited resources to access cutting-edge technology and participate in global efforts to combat environmental degradation.

Policy Recommendations for Open-Source AI

Proposal: Government Policies to Promote Open-Source Development

To fully realize the potential of open-source AI, governments must play an active role in creating policies that encourage and support open-source development. Without appropriate policy frameworks, there is a risk that AI technologies will become concentrated in the hands of a few large companies, leading to monopolistic control and limiting the benefits of AI to a select group of stakeholders. By promoting open-source AI, governments can ensure that AI technologies remain transparent, accessible, and accountable to the public.

One of the key reasons for encouraging open-source AI development is to prevent **monopolistic control** of AI technologies. Currently, a handful of tech giants dominate the AI industry, controlling vast amounts of data, computational resources, and talent. This concentration of power raises concerns about competition, innovation, and the ethical use of AI. Without interventions from governments, these companies may continue to expand their influence, creating a digital divide where only the wealthiest countries and corporations can fully benefit from AI advancements.

Governments can counter this trend by implementing policies that **incentivize open-source AI development**. These policies could include providing funding and grants for open-source AI projects, offering tax breaks to companies that contribute to open-source platforms, and creating public-private partnerships to support open-source AI research. Additionally, governments could establish **regulatory frameworks** that require AI systems used in critical industries—such as healthcare, finance, and public services—to be open-source or to undergo independent audits for transparency and accountability.

An existing example of such a framework is the **European Union's AI Act**, which is currently being developed to regulate the use of AI within the EU. The AI Act includes provisions that promote transparency, accountability, and fairness in AI development, with a focus on high-risk AI applications that could affect people's rights and safety. The Act encourages the use of open-source AI by mandating transparency in the algorithms used for critical decision-making processes and requiring companies to disclose how their AI systems are trained, tested, and deployed. This level of transparency helps mitigate the risks associated with proprietary AI systems, which are often opaque and difficult to scrutinize.

The **EU AI Act** also promotes public oversight of AI systems, ensuring that governments, independent researchers, and civil society organizations have access to the information they need to evaluate the ethical and societal impacts of AI. By setting clear rules for AI development and deployment, the EU AI Act serves as a model for other governments seeking to regulate AI in ways that promote transparency and accountability. Similar frameworks could be adopted by other countries, ensuring that open-source AI plays a central role in the development of AI technologies that are safe, fair, and accessible to all.

Example: The EU AI Act and Its Role in Promoting Transparency

The **EU AI Act** provides a concrete example of how governments can promote open-source AI development through regulatory frameworks. By requiring transparency and accountability in the development of high-risk AI systems, the Act encourages the use of open-source models and helps prevent the monopolistic control of AI technologies. This regulatory approach ensures that AI systems are subject to public oversight and that their development is aligned with ethical and societal values.

Shaping the Future of AI Through Collaboration and Policy

The future of AI development will be defined by how well the global community embraces collaboration and transparency. Open-source AI provides a unique opportunity to create an inclusive and equitable AI ecosystem, where people from all over the world can contribute to and benefit from AI technologies. By fostering cross-border initiatives and developing AI solutions to address global challenges like climate change, public health, and poverty, open-source AI can help ensure that AI serves the common good.

However, realizing the full potential of open-source AI requires concerted efforts from governments to create policies that support and encourage open-source development. By implementing regulatory frameworks like the EU AI Act and offering financial incentives for open-source AI projects, governments can prevent the monopolization of AI technologies and promote transparency and accountability. As AI continues to shape the future, these policy measures will be essential for ensuring that AI development remains ethical, fair, and accessible to all.

In this way, open-source AI is not just a technical model—it is a global movement that, with the right policies in place, can drive sustainable innovation, foster international cooperation, and address the most pressing challenges facing humanity today. By investing in open-source AI, governments and organizations can shape a future where AI technologies are developed transparently and shared equitably across borders, ensuring that the benefits of AI are available to everyone.

Conclusion

As we stand at the cusp of an AI-driven future, the question of how artificial intelligence is developed, regulated, and deployed has never been more critical. Throughout this book, we have explored the complexities of AI development and the ethical, societal, and economic challenges that arise from proprietary systems controlled by a handful of powerful entities. We have also examined how open-source AI offers a promising alternative—one that promotes transparency, accountability, collaboration, and innovation. In this conclusion, we will recap the key arguments presented, reflect on the future of AI, and issue a call to action for all stakeholders to advocate for open-source AI development to ensure a responsible and equitable technological future.

Summary of Key Arguments

The central theme of this book has been the argument that **open-source AI** is the key to a more **transparent, ethical, and unbiased** future for artificial intelligence. Open-source AI, by its very nature, invites contributions from a diverse community of developers, researchers, and ethicists. This transparency helps mitigate many of the ethical challenges that proprietary AI systems face, such as bias, security risks, and the lack of public oversight. Throughout the chapters, we have highlighted several crucial reasons why open-source AI is the best path forward for responsible AI development:

1. **Transparency**: Open-source AI allows for full visibility into the inner workings of algorithms, data, and decision-making processes. Unlike proprietary AI, which often operates as a "black box," open-source AI ensures that anyone—researchers, developers, policymakers, or the public—can audit and scrutinize AI systems for potential flaws or biases. This transparency is crucial for fostering trust in AI systems, particularly in sectors like healthcare, criminal justice, and finance, where decisions made by AI can have profound impacts on individuals' lives.
2. **Bias Reduction**: AI systems developed behind closed doors often suffer from biases that reflect the limited perspectives of their developers. These biases, whether related to race, gender, or socioeconomic status, can perpetuate systemic inequalities. Open-source AI, by inviting contributions from a global, diverse community, reduces the risk of such biases going unnoticed. The collaborative nature of open-source development ensures that AI systems are audited and improved continuously, leading to fairer and more equitable outcomes.
3. **Ethical Oversight**: As discussed in previous sections, many private companies struggle to implement effective ethical oversight due to conflicts of interest or a lack of independence in their ethics boards. Open-source AI, on the other hand, creates a platform for **independent ethical audits** by global experts. This continuous ethical monitoring ensures that AI systems are developed with a focus on human rights, fairness, and accountability, rather than profit motives.
4. **Innovation and Collaboration**: Open-source AI fosters a collaborative environment where innovation can thrive. By sharing code, data, and insights freely, developers from all over the world can contribute to solving complex challenges, from climate change to healthcare delivery. This collaborative spirit not only accelerates technological progress but also ensures that AI solutions are developed with a broader range of needs and contexts in mind.

Each of these arguments demonstrates why open-source AI is not just a technical choice but an ethical and societal imperative. By embracing open-source development, we can build AI systems that reflect our collective values and serve the public good.

Final Thoughts on the Future of AI

Looking ahead, the long-term benefits of open-source AI are clear. As AI becomes more embedded in everyday life, from healthcare and education to transportation and governance, the need for systems that are **trustworthy, transparent, and equitable** will only grow. Open-source AI provides a model for achieving these goals, ensuring that the development of AI remains a **shared, global effort** that prioritizes the public interest over private gain.

One of the most important long-term benefits of open-source AI is its potential to drive **sustainable innovation**. The collaborative nature of open-source development allows for the rapid exchange of ideas, the identification of best practices, and the continuous improvement of AI models. This democratization of AI innovation ensures that the latest technological advances are accessible to a wide range of industries and communities, not just a select few large corporations. In fields like **medicine**, for instance, open-source AI can lead to breakthroughs in diagnostics, treatment, and patient care that benefit populations worldwide, particularly in low-resource settings.

Moreover, as open-source AI continues to evolve, it will play a critical role in ensuring that **AI systems remain accountable**. In an age where AI is increasingly used to make decisions about everything from hiring to lending and criminal sentencing, it is essential that these systems are transparent and subject to continuous oversight. Open-source AI provides the framework for this kind of accountability, giving stakeholders the tools they need to ensure that AI systems are ethical, fair, and aligned with societal values.

In short, the future of AI development will depend heavily on how well we can harness the collaborative potential of open-source models. By leveraging the strengths of open-source AI—transparency, inclusivity, and ethical oversight—we can ensure that AI technologies are developed in ways that benefit all of humanity, rather than exacerbating inequalities or serving narrow corporate interests.

Call to Action

To realize this vision for the future of AI, it is crucial that all stakeholders—**companies, governments, and the public**—take an active role in advocating for open-source AI development. The responsibility for shaping the future of AI cannot rest solely with private corporations; it requires a collective effort to ensure that AI is developed responsibly and with the public good in mind.

- **Companies** should embrace open-source AI as a means of fostering innovation, improving transparency, and building trust with consumers and stakeholders. By contributing to open-source AI projects and adopting open-source principles in their own AI development, companies can help ensure that AI systems are more inclusive, ethical, and accountable. In industries like healthcare and finance, where trust is paramount, open-source AI can provide a competitive advantage by demonstrating a commitment to fairness and transparency.
- **Governments** have a critical role to play in creating policies that support open-source AI development. By offering funding, tax incentives, and regulatory frameworks that prioritize transparency and accountability, governments can ensure that AI technologies are developed in ways that serve the public interest. As we have seen with initiatives like the **EU AI Act**, governments can lead the way in establishing the ethical and legal standards that will shape the future of AI. It is essential that governments work together to create a global regulatory framework that promotes open-source AI and prevents the monopolization of AI technologies by a few dominant players.
- **The public** also has a role in advocating for open-source AI. As AI becomes increasingly integrated into everyday life, individuals and communities must demand greater transparency and accountability from the companies and institutions that

develop and deploy AI systems. By supporting open-source AI projects, participating in public consultations on AI policy, and advocating for ethical AI development, the public can help ensure that AI technologies are aligned with societal values and that their benefits are shared equitably.

In conclusion, the future of AI development will be shaped by the choices we make today. Open-source AI offers a powerful model for ensuring that AI technologies are developed in ways that are transparent, ethical, and fair. By embracing open-source principles and fostering collaboration across borders, we can build a future where AI serves the public good and contributes to a more just and equitable world. It is up to all of us—companies, governments, and individuals—to advocate for this vision and to ensure that AI is developed responsibly for the benefit of all.

Disclaimer:

"This book was created with the assistance of artificial intelligence (AI) tools, which were used to organize information and further develop insights. While AI contributed to the drafting process, the content was carefully written, reviewed, edited, and refined by the author to ensure accuracy, coherence, and relevance. I have taken great care to validate the information presented and to align it with current research and best practices in AI ethics, development, and open-source collaboration."

"Please note that any perspectives or recommendations provided in this book represent the authors' insights and interpretations and are intended to inform and encourage thoughtful engagement with AI's role in society."

www.ingramcontent.com/pod-product-compliance
Lightning Source LLC
Chambersburg PA
CBHW031518210526
45464CB00007B/2967